1

SEDUCTION
Pleasing Women Sexually

by Branch Isole

Copyright © 2013
Printed in the United States of America

Seduction
Pleasing Women Sexually
by Branch Isole

Library of Congress Control Number: 2011903376
ISBN 978-0982658598
eBook ISBN 9780983574583

 **MANA'O PUBLISHING**

Home of the VOYEURISTIC POET

Manao Publishing
Hampton, VA 23666

Order copies of this book at:
www.branchisole.com
www.manaopublishing.com

Seduction
Pleasing Women Sexually

Written and presented to promote
healthy sexuality between consenting adults.

"The worst sex you ever have
should be fantastic"

TABLE OF CONTENTS

Introduction

Chapters

Epilogue

Introduction

As a younger man I had a female friend in San Diego, California. One day she called informing me her father had died and the details of removing property from his home had been left for her to accomplish. She asked if I would help with this task and a date was soon scheduled. When we had finished, she told me that I could have anything in the house as gratitude for my assistance.

While boxing many of the smaller items, I had noticed a stack of older magazines and made mention of it to her. She said when she unpacked the boxes and came across the set of periodicals she would forward them to me. Several weeks later they arrived in the mail. While leafing through them on a Saturday afternoon I came across a set of loose papers, which had been placed inside one of the magazines. As these papers pertained to sexuality and the long practiced techniques of history's legendary Lotharios, being a man I read these papers with great interest. It was not what I expected. It was much more. More than that, it works. Most importantly, it will work for you!

The information I am about to share will turn you into a sexual dynamo; a Don Juan, Casanova and Cyrano de Bergerac all rolled into one. Follow these steps and you will soon become sexually desirable to every woman with whom you are romantically

intimate. Read, learn and practice these twelve chapters and you'll soon discover both you and your partners will enjoy each other more totally and fully. With this information you will unleash the addictive sexuality which resides deep within every woman. All she is waiting for is the man who can help it surface, allow it to come out, and guide it to fruition. This book will help you to become that man.
'The lover every woman wants.'

~Branch Isole

"It's one thing to shoot a man,
quite another to cast aspersions
upon his lovemaking skills."

~Teresa Medeiros,
The Vampire Who Loved Me

"Tell him I've been too fucking busy,
or vice versa."

~Dorothy Parker

Chapter 1: Having Someone Sexually Lusting for You

"The greatest levels of sexual pleasure are attained when both partners are at their highest physical and mental stages of excitement."

You are about to discover the secrets of sexual irresistibility shared by the world's great and legendary lovers. More than this you will learn the ways of bringing out your own deepest, richest male sexuality. The relationship between these two is no coincidence.

In order to bring the woman you are intimate with under your intoxicating spell, she must first believe that you are totally devoted to her pleasure. To achieve this shared sense of excitement and sexual energy, you must lose yourself *in her pleasure*. You must become swept up in it, you must experience it and you must feel it as your own. Aware that you are not holding back in your giving and your desires to please her, she will be free to express her own physical enjoyment with uninhibited sounds, movements, words and acts, which will then drive you to even higher levels of excitement and enjoyment. Where will this ascending spiral of lust and heated sexuality end? It will culminate in a rapture the two of you will share. Your new sexual journey together will be beyond words or past imaginations.

After this sexually charged experience, more than ever before in her life she will be overwhelmed by the intensity of the lovemaking you two shared. You will become her fulfillment as a lover and the one man who can satisfy her sexual needs, both conscious and subconscious.

Once with you will not be enough. She will crave you again and again. Nothing less than you inside of her will accommodate the new satiated level of lovemaking she now desires. Her being and all her senses will become attune to you in a permanent state of excitement, which nothing else or any other man will be able to appease.

Her entire body will become sensitized to you; the sight of you, your smell, your touch. Even the thought of you will wash over her like a powerful flood of memory sensations as she recalls the ecstasy she experienced having had sex with you.

Like a starving person salivating at the sight of food, like the alcoholic seeing a glass of whiskey, like the casino gambler eyeing stacks of chips, like the smoker at the sight of a newly lit cigarette; she will feel an uncontrollable and overpowering urge to experience you sexually again. She will remember the pleasure she now associates with you, your body and your lovemaking.

If she cannot have you she will become frustrated, desperate and inconsolable. She may turn to substitutes such as self-pleasuring, toys and devices, even other men but nothing will work. Surrogates will only serve to increase her pangs and longings for the one and only thing, which will satisfy her new lust filled desires: You. She will become sexually addicted to you.

A state of permanent sexual excitation over one man can become a true addiction but this is *not* meant to be a negative condition. It can become negative if you use what you are about to learn to seduce and abandon. You should know however, that used correctly it is a good, healthy and desirable pattern of sexual behavior between two adults. In fact, the ability to be and become sexually addicted to your partner is one of the cornerstones of long term relationships.

Mutual sexual lusting is one of the prime motivators why men and women pair off and then stay together as partners for years. A healthy and mutual sexual lusting for one another is part of the glue and physical bonding that continues to hold couples together. Without a shared sexual lusting for each other, situations such as adultery, depression, anger, fear, frustration, divorce and/or chronic unhappiness may result.

With a healthy sexual lust for each other, life together for both partners can become a passionate love affair that only grows and intensifies over time. Your love life together will become as intense as any true addiction but unlike many others, this one will be good for your health, your body and your soul.

Despite its deep rooted nature in the biology of the human species, long term mutual sexual compatibility seems to be the exception rather than the rule in most contemporary relationships. In modern societies a mutually exclusive yet all-consuming and tempestuous sex life over the long term is considered to be so rare as to be unusual. The norm of an average sexual relationship on course, (uninterrupted by events such as war or unexpected separations) tends to run about six months of full-on lust filled emotional and physically intense sexual heat and behavior followed by approximately two years of continuing passion. This pattern generally slides steadily into an ever dwindling reduction of sexual interest and activity with the suspension of courting and dating infatuation.

Career and work demands or the arrival of children with their needs may curtail dramatically continued sexual lusting. With less and less time and attention for each other partners may find themselves in situations where their sex life becomes more rote and routine, rather than expanded enticement.

This is a sexual tragedy and totally unnecessary. In these twelve chapters you will discover how to prevent your sexual relationship from deteriorating and dying. You will also learn how to keep your sexual relationship on a new and ever increasing plane. If your relationship is already in a state of steady decline due to age or routine, you now have the opportunity to rekindle the earlier passions you and your partner once knew and experienced. They *can* exist again on a regular basis.

If you are still dating and actively playing the field in regard to sexual relationships, by applying the steps presented here you will learn how to sexually addict a woman from the very beginning, even from your first night of intimacy together. Those currently in monogamous relationships can use these techniques to restart the fires of heat and passion with their current ladies. Where you go from here and how high you ascend is up to you.

"When a man goes on a date he wonders if he is
going to get lucky.
A woman already knows."

~Frederike Ryder

Chapter 2: Understanding Female Sexuality
*"The first and foremost facet in this understanding
is to know that there are profound sexual differences
between men and women, beyond the obvious."*

One of the biggest mistakes men make and the single
most important difference separating the majority of
men from the sought after lovers, is most men project
their own genital centered responses onto the women
with whom they are making love. Men mistakenly
presume a woman is feeling exactly the same as they
are. *She isn't!*

The quick arousal, fast intercourse, orgasm and end
of sex sequence, which is all too normal and
satisfying for a man, can be deadly for a woman and
guarantees *NOT* to fulfill her.

In order to create the desired sexual attachment you
are attempting to establish with the lady in your life
it is incumbent to more fully understand the general
nature of sexuality in women. To begin with, male
sexuality is for the most part genitally focused,
meaning it is primarily physically centered in the

region of the penis and testicles. For women, their sexuality is much more diffused. While orgasms in women as with men centers in the genitals, a woman's sexuality *can* encompass the entirety of her body and being.

Linked to the essential biological differences in male and female sexual response is the fact women are sexually superior to men in a vast number of ways. It is of utmost importance that you as a male understand and accept this. This has been well known throughout the ages in the many societies which have recognized women's greater sexual prowess. Men in these societies have often been threatened by, and have made attempts both veiled and overt, to try and subdue it.

For example, 'the Crusaders' of the Middle Ages locked up their wives' genitalia with chastity belts and other devices when they went off to war. These 'Warriors of the Cross' believed nothing less than a solid metal barricade could or would contain their women's sex drives and ward off other interested parties. There was always a concern that men not involved in long distance efforts on behalf of church or king, could not be trusted and were readily available to take advantage of, or rape the women at home. At a minimum, this was believed to be a good and rational reason to impose chastity restrictions upon their women. They also thought such devices would succeed in stemming the tide of a woman's desire to be accessed and filled in her man's absence. Likewise many Muslim sultans and sheiks employed eunuchs to guard their harems. Clearly these were men who believed there might have been opportunities whereby their women were only to be trusted around other men who had been castrated.

During both the nineteenth and twentieth centuries, many women commonly suffered having their clitoris forcibly removed surgically or were given other medical procedures to abate their sexual desires and the possibilities of promiscuity. Today in many countries multiple numbers of women have had their genitals forcibly and/or severely mutilated to prevent them from experiencing or fulfilling their own potential sexual pleasures.

On the other hand, in many ancient oriental cultures there was and is a different and often better understanding and acceptance about women's greater sexual capacities. While many oriental sages professed and urged men to conserve their semen and have as few orgasms as possible believing each orgasm shortened a man's life, they contrarily encouraged women to have as many orgasms as possible. To assist women in achieving these multiple orgasmic opportunities without depleting their men, a host of beautiful and ingenious sex toys were created to help women satisfy themselves as often as they wished, needed or wanted.

What is this superior female sexual prowess and power, and how can you harness it to addict your woman to you? Superior female sexual power simply means women have a much greater and more extensive sexual capacity than most men do. That is, they can achieve and enjoy multiple and often times more intense orgasms than a man. In fact, for most women under the right conditions and with the right partner, their orgasmic power is virtually unlimited. If successfully taken to a high sexual plateau a woman can often have one orgasm after another until she is unable to continue or forced to stop by sheer physical exhaustion. Women have been closely observed in clinical laboratory settings to have as many as sixty orgasms in a row, each one powerful and distinct. Even falling short of this extreme it is not out of the question and completely within the realm of possibility for the average woman to have two, three, four or more orgasms during a typical sexual encounter.

A man's orgasmic proclivity is more limited. The average male normally has one orgasm and after he ejaculates is often finished for a substantial amount of time. While some men have trained themselves to have more than one single event orgasm before and in conjunction with their ejaculation this is still the exception to the rule. In the event of such 'staying' power, the quality and duration of multiple orgasms in these individual men are still incomparable to those of most women in the general public. Not only are women definitely more orgasmic than men, they can experience three distinct types of orgasms, all with varieties of different associated sensations. The three kinds of female orgasms are; clitoral, vaginal and a clitoral/vaginal combination. Also unlike men, the more orgasms a woman has, the more intensely orgasmic she may become.

If we were to chart the curve of a woman's sexual excitement under the right conditions and with the right partner, it would rise upward in an ever ascending line until it reached a continuous peak that might last for hours. This heightened excitement and state of response could then provide for and promote within the woman a propensity of extending the possibility of being readily available to experience orgasms for days. It is small wonder that many men have felt threatened by this mighty sexual force and have an overwhelming need to try and control or eliminate it, rather than be vanquished by it.

Given this power of a woman's greater sexual endurance the question then becomes, "How do you as a man, keep up with and satisfy her?" Simple. By recognizing this reality and by *not* attempting to keep up with her at all! Instead, you must learn to use her superior orgasmic capacity to give her as many satisfying orgasms as she wants and desires, without depleting yourself.

Even today most women choose to return again and again to the man who exudes the greatest sexual confidence and power. That is, he who best satisfies her voracious sexual appetite once it has been awakened. The true key to lovemaking is to understand and learn how to use this power to heighten the sexual pleasures of both partners.

If you can do this then you are sexually aware and cognizant indeed. In other words, if you will recognize your woman's sexual prowess, power and superiority, you can learn to command and control it much the same way you steer a powerful car.

"Sex is as important as eating or drinking and we ought to allow one appetite to be satisfied with as little restraint or false modesty as the other."

~Marquis de Sade,
L'Histoire de Juliette

Chapter 3: The Power of Addiction

"We have all known smokers who have quit after years of smoking, only to return to their nicotine habit when confronted by a particular situation or stimulus."

To successfully addict a woman to a point of complete lusting, you must fulfill the requirement and actions of any addiction. You must first satisfy a powerful recurring need and then you must satisfy it so well that no other substitute will suffice or do. You are surely familiar with this concept and how it works in more well-known addictions, such as drugs and alcohol. As with any other addiction, sexual lusting satisfies both a physical and a psychological craving. After a while the person becomes "hooked" or dependent upon the specific source. If the source is withdrawn the hooked person experiences disruptive and sometimes painful withdrawal symptoms. As strong as the physical dependency may be, it is the psychological dependency which in many cases is the 'hardest to kick.'

For example, generally speaking because of the biological magnificence of the physical human body and its capabilities, a cigarette smoker is free of physical withdrawal symptoms in about two weeks after they quit smoking. The psychological cravings and dependency however, may continue for months, years or even longer.

The principle of sexual lust works in exactly the same way. The 'substance' (you) satisfies a powerful recurring need (your lady's physical need and psychological desire for sexual pleasure) and subsequently you satisfy her so well that no other substitute will do. When a woman finds such a man, one who can totally satisfy her in this sexual way, she can become immersed in him. His smell, his touch, his sight, his pleasuring and loving ways. Similar to any other kind of addiction, the more she needs him and the more she is satisfied; the greater the need becomes and the stronger her urge to fill it.

There is one enormous and perhaps essential difference between your woman's sexual lusting and any other compulsion: her sexual need is healthy for her in both mind and body. Why? Physically, she cannot overdose on sex. The more sexual activity she has with you, the more tensions and stress in both her life and body are relieved and reduced. The greater her body's production of endorphins, the greater relaxation and sense of calm she will have. Meaning sex with you will give her a natural high.

If, as the song goes "It's you and nobody else but you" she will most likely not engage in high risk sexual behavior with other partners. More importantly, a strong monogamous sexual relationship is one of the foundations upon which healthy and happy unions and marriages form and thrive. Mutual sexual lusting can be fulfilling, intimate and help promote a long term relationship between two people.

At this point you may be thinking or saying, "Not every woman has such a powerful sexual need." Perhaps. You may believe your woman "Is not really passionate or interested in sex." Or maybe you say, "She's not even capable of being lust filled." Fear Not! Every woman has a powerful sexual need deep within the inner recesses of her being. Not every woman however, is necessarily aware of it. Even if she is, she may not know exactly what she wants sexually. If she does know, your part is easier. If she doesn't know, it's up to you to help her find out and discover it.

A cautionary note here; for success in the techniques which will be specified and explained in the following steps, we are presuming the woman in question is of normal sexual responsiveness. If she is unresponsive due to extenuating physical or mental circumstances, there may be a variety of different causes. Possibilities may include psycho-pathology, which result in sexual repression(s) and/or "frigid" behavior.

If curable, these conditions may only respond to extensive psycho-therapies and/or sex therapies. Other causes may be repression from negative anti-sexual conditioning through up-bringing and/or family dynamics or cultural sources such as religion, personal and/or social taboos and mores. With some women there may be a number of different physical or psychological problems requiring professional medical attention.

This series addresses itself to women not suffering from the above stated repressions, physical/mental issues and/or medical problems and who have healthy sexual responses, which need only be heightened and developed. The steps and techniques which will be described in the balance of this book may aide the socially or religiously repressed woman, if she is aware and cognizant she is repressing issues, is readily eager to free herself, is willing to experiment and has healthy sexual responses lying dormant beneath the repression. For example, an apparently religious or socially repressed 'rigid or frigid' woman who successfully masturbates, however guilt laden such an activity may be, is a good candidate for a healthy sexual relationship.

It should be reiterated here; the power of sexuality can be used for good *or* for ill. For good, it can bind two people together in a joyful, healthy and ever-growing intimacy. When used by a man interested only in making conquest after conquest, a "lady-killer" "womanizer" or "philanderer" can undoubtedly cause more harm than good. How *you* use this power and responsibility is up to you.

"Sex...or lack thereof ...is at the center
of everyone's identity, and once you've cracked
someone's desires, you understand them in full."

~Arianne Cohen,
Marie Claire Magazine, March 2008

Chapter 4: The Five General Rules of Sexual Lusting
"Know that the hotter she gets, the hotter she will get."

Rule 1: Tease Her Mercilessly.

It has been said that a woman has a thousand erogenous zones, while a man has but one. To this statement there may be some solid evidence and valid truth. When a man has an erection he is ready (or thinks he is ready) for sexual intercourse. His first desire is to immediately have his penis and testicles touched, fondled or grabbed by parts of the female anatomy. Women for the most part are just the opposite. This is the one area where women are significantly and biologically different from men. They do not want their genitals touched until *after* they are highly aroused and normally speaking, their arousal state takes longer than does a man's. Making things even more complicated, there are varying degrees of female arousal along a quite lengthy continuum *and* this can vary from female to female.

A woman may be wet and swollen but still not be completely ready for vaginal penetration and intercourse. Or she may be ready for intercourse, but not as ready as she could be! Their sexual stimuli areas are more subtle and complex and as such, women usually need to lubricate from several different genital areas. In order for a woman to enjoy maximum arousal sensations, her outer genital lips need to swell. Her vagina will also need to swell and soften to more easily admit the man's penis in a welcoming embrace with a minimum of resistance and irritation.

What you want to do is bring her to *maximum readiness*. Maximum readiness can be described as a state of such intense arousal that she *must* have an orgasm or she will feel a sense of discomfort. At the maximum readiness stage she will be incapable of keeping still. Only when she is at this level of maximum arousal can she enjoy all the pleasure and satisfaction she desires. This is the stage to which you want to take her. The question is, *How*?

This is a level of true ecstasy, one whereby her orgasm will exceed any other bodily pleasure or associated discomfort. Once she has experienced it, she will crave it again and again. And since you are the one who took her to this place of delirious pleasure, she will now believe you are the only one who knows how to take her there again. She will beg and plead; she will do anything, even to a point of using you ruthlessly to satisfy her desires. To reach this stage in your lovemaking, she must ascend to higher and higher levels of arousal. These kinds of heightened stages of arousal take time, skill and patience from you.

In a word; *Teasing*.

To assist you in understanding this concept of teasing and its importance, think of *her entire body* as one erogenous zone. From this moment on, know and understand; her genitals are the *last place* you should touch! First are her cheeks, hair, lips, arms, feet, breasts, back; anyplace other than her genitals. Kiss her, gently touch her and sensually caress any and all skin on her body *except* her genitals. All your efforts will eventually lead to and find their way to the wetness between her legs.

If you follow this first step, by the time you reach that cherished spot, she should already be extremely wet and swollen. At that moment, even the lightest brushing against or teasing touch of her clitoris should send her shivering. Is she now ready? NO! Now the teasing and pleasing really begins and intensifies.

Rule Two: Her Pleasure *Always* Comes First.

If you have not discovered by now you soon will: the greatest thrill in all of sex is driving the *other person* wild with heightened sensual and sexual excitement. Conversely, one of the biggest turn-offs is to be with a sexual robot who stays personally cold and detached.

I remember the story of one of my fraternity brothers in college who managed to bed down one of the most popular and beautiful women on campus. As the story goes, he was working as hard as he could, penetrating her deeply when she absently said, "I think my check book is overdrawn."

Remember, *you* can be satisfied more or less with the simple repetition of your penis' thrust and parry. She *cannot*. You must learn and know how to become a complete tool of her sexual desires. She must know for a certainty that she has the uninterrupted luxury of time with you. If she wants a slow teasing lovemaking session with you that takes hours to build to completion, she must know that you are gladly willing to give it to her. If on the other hand, she wants you for immediate sexual intercourse and gratification, you will give her that as well.

Her body's close proximity to your penis is probably enough to adequately excite you into becoming hard with an accompanying bead of semen on the tip of your penis, but alas, not so the other way around (yet). Therefore, to properly entice her you must have the control of a combat fighter pilot and the patience of Job.

Now that we have established she should always be allowed and encouraged to come first, what about you? Is there a "you" in all this lovemaking for hours and days on end? Absolutely! One of the phenomenal aspects of every woman's sexuality is that she has a 'built-in' genetic component and essential part to her nature; *giving you pleasure*. One of the crucial weapons in your new sexual arsenal is your ability to lose control in her hands. She wants to experience the thrill and power of turning you into a helpless mass of writhing ecstasy. Give this to her and you will be rewarded tenfold.

Rule Three: Allow and Encourage Her to Let Go.

Women, because of social training and conditioning have historically had their sexuality repressed, suppressed and oppressed in male dominated societies. Nevertheless, nature and biology are overwhelmingly powerful and despite all attempts by societies, religions, cultures and institutions throughout the ages, generally speaking women are still profoundly hot-blooded creatures. (As mentioned earlier, there may be exceptions for women with serious pathologies.)

Women know this about themselves. They admit it to themselves and to each other much more freely than men do. They have learned to keep hidden from men much of this information about themselves and as a result, most or all of their passion.

Women have often been pressured to play a virtuous role within society, which has then burdened them with penalties, ostracism, disdain and even imprisonment or death for expressing their sexuality openly or aggressively. As stated prior, many societies' members feel threatened by explicit female sexuality.

If you want to unleash the volcano that is your lady's sexuality you must encourage and allow her to be herself and express it openly to and with you. This is not as easy as it sounds. This means *you* must be equally free and uninhibited sexually. You must not be judgmental.

Once you have let this cat out of the bag, you may be shocked (and so may she) by the behaviors and the desires that explode from her. If however, you are sexually free enough to handle this, the rewards for both of you will be astonishing.

If you ready and willing to risk it, this then is what you must do: *Show and tell* her you love it when she loses control and is totally herself.

Be free and uninhibited yourself in your words and actions.

Reveal intimacies about your own sexuality, desires and fantasies. Remember, this will make you vulnerable, but with this knowledge she will not feel alone or uncomfortable when exposing to you more intimate details about herself.

Make *talk* an important part of your sexual encounters and lovemaking. This means not only 'talking dirty' (which is a natural and great turn-on for many) but also by talking lover to lover about what feels good to you and by asking and allowing her to feel comfortable enough to express openly what feels good to and for her.

Show her by your body language you are not uptight or nervous. Lavish upon her entire body inch by inch; kisses and caresses with lips, tongue, fingers and hands. Freely sigh, moan and make sounds out loud. Take lascivious pleasure in her sweats, secretions and body fluids against your skin and on your body.

Be delighted when she takes the initiative and experiments with or on you; lie back and let her ravish all she wants.

Never refuse her sexual overtures. Even if you are not in the mood, even if you can't get an erection, you can still pleasure and satisfy her.

Rule Four: Sex is with the Heart and Mind. Your Penis is just a Tool.

If your habit is to use your penis in a hard or punishing way, or if your penis has become a weapon instead of an instrument of joy and pleasure for either or both of you, you are making war, not love. Once you recognize your penis is only a tool, a sexual 'material expression' of your mind and heart, you will also realize it is not the only tool you have at your disposal and in your repertoire. Other objects can and will express your lovemaking and are capable of giving her fulfilling sexual pleasure; whether they are hands, tongue, vibrators, toys or dildos.

When you finally understand this, you will be able to make love for indefinite periods of time and do it successfully non-stop. With this in mind, if your primary tool; your penis, is temporarily spent, you can still keep up with even the most insatiable wanting woman.

Rule Five: Once is Only the Beginning *and* Never Enough.

The more you tease her with your hands, lips, tongue and genitals, the higher her state of arousal will become and remain, until you finally relent and have sexual intercourse with her. The higher her arousal level and the hotter she becomes, the more quickly she will become sexually aroused again. She will become even more sexually responsive with each succeeding intercourse event the two of you share.

With repeated stimulation of her genitals, she will continue to become more intensely sensitive. She will be more aroused with each subsequent and satisfying encounter and will expectantly anticipate the next opportunity and progressive stages of arousal.

Your ultimate goal is to have marathon sex. This means you should not limit your sexual encounters to a single session, but extend them over a period of hours and possibly days. You may well be rewarded by the discovery that the morning after such a marathon session, your lady will wake up in a great sexual heat and demand immediate intercourse with no foreplay whatsoever. She will already be swollen, wet, ready and more excited than you have seen her even after hours of foreplay. Don't be fooled, her "instant heat" is not a new event; it is actually an extension of the culmination of hours of sexual activity the two of you shared the night before.

If and when she should attain this "give me intercourse immediately" stage, you will know she is now sexually lusting for you. The more often she is brought to and experiences this stage, the more amorously addicted to you she will become.

Naturally no one can, wants to, or has time to have this kind of marathon sex on a daily basis. However, you should try whenever possible to make marathon sex a regular part of your current and future sex life.

Perhaps once or twice a month, or once every two months depending on your age, desires, situation and stamina. The amount or number of times is not the important aspect here. What's important is that she now knows she will always have another marathon session to look forward to in the near future. Remember she wants sexual pleasure as much as you do.

The prospect of marathon sex may be disheartening to you at first. After all, she can keep going indefinitely and you can't right? Wrong! You can't only if your definition of having sex is that of Ex-President Bill Clinton's statement about his "improper relationship" (sexual encounters) with Monica Lewinski; "It's only sex if it is vaginal intercourse by penile penetration."

Today, the definition of sex is certainly much broader. For women, its sex if her body is penetrated and gives pleasure and/or orgasms to you or her. This includes not only by your penis, but also by your hands, mouth, pelvis, tongue, sex toys/devices, objects or anything else that the two of you can think of and agree upon. So by all means use this definition, not Bill Clinton's. If your penis is spent for the moment, get busy with the other now available and ready parts of your body and keep busy pleasing until she drops from sheer and utter exhaustion.

You may discover it takes very little energy for you to move your finger, thumb or tongue back and forth on her clitoris. Not only that, you should be able to do this to and for her, for hours. Either way, she will be happily writhing around in pleasurable ecstasy and acceptance.

These then are the five general rules of sexual lusting. Next we will look at their specific applications and techniques.

"When it comes to being a good lover,
a guy has to ask a girl what she wants
and be willing to give it to her."

~Jenna Jameson

Chapter 5: Get Her Totally Ready For Intercourse

"Pleasure Techniques for You to Use. With three basic pleasure techniques (Chapters 5, 6 & 7) you can sexually satisfy any woman, even in a single or first encounter."

Pleasure Technique # 1

At this point in your sexual life, can you even imagine kissing without ever going below the neck could bring any woman to a point where she is totally ready for sexual intercourse with you? Probably not, right? Wrong!

If this is a foreign concept to you, it shouldn't be. Can you recall those youthful nights of "making out" when you could kiss for hours? Yes? Most likely you finished those 'necking sessions' with a painful case of "blue balls" as it was commonly known, but had it been worth it? Of course! And what about her? How did she leave those heavy kissing and petting sessions? You probably never gave it a second thought did you? Well you should have because despite the focus of your male frustration, reinforced by the fact most often it was the female who put the brakes on sexual situations and proceedings; she was probably just as physically strung out as you were.

You probably left those marathon kissing entanglements with an enormous and aching erectile "hard on". However, she left with an equally aching engorgement of her entire genital area inside as well as outside, which was evident by her wet panties. In other words by the time the two of you stopped necking, you were both in maximum physical readiness for sexual intercourse. There is absolutely no reason for this to have changed. If kissing could be such an exciting and passionate form of sexual foreplay then, it can be now.

It's true as people grow in relationships they tend to go through a process of desensitization. That first kiss, that first touch of a breast, the first penetration and experience of sexual intercourse with a woman is incomparable, exciting and vividly memorable. The problem is with each succeeding sexual encounter, the intensity becomes a little less infatuating and a little more familiar. Nevertheless, kissing is still the most elementary part of human sexual contact. The thing to remember here is, you can still use kissing to excite your thirty, forty or fifty year old lady as much as you did and in the same way as when you were sixteen.

Pleasure Technique # 1 is the adult version of the kissing-to-a-frenzy experience: The key to sexually addicting a woman through kissing alone is that you understand; kissing *mimics* sexual intercourse. Think of yourself as the inserter (Tab A) and your lady as the receiver (Slot B). In kissing, as with sexual intercourse the man inserts his tongue (long and full like his penis) in and around his lady's wet and warm mouth while she is receiving and sucking just as her vaginal muscles do. This fact is true whether she is aware of the activity or not. It is your consciousness and acceptance of it, which will now give you the power of sexual addiction.

If you are kissing her correctly, you will be giving her the oral equivalence of transcendent ecstatic sexual intercourse. This will also give her a preview and the knowledge of what actual vaginal intercourse with you will be like. You will be imprinting this image upon her psyche and planting seeds somatically and experientially of her now knowing you physically, so both her mind and body will be more receptive. Intense desires will awaken within her so that she will begin to become impatient for sexual intercourse, the same way she did in the back seat of your car parked at lovers' lane. However, you will NOT give it to her! In order to accomplish and satisfy her impending and needed sexual release you will continue to tease and torment her until she begins to beg for your penis.

This step will be described shortly but for now, this is exactly what you are to do in applying your kissing technique:

Take your time!
Take your time!
Take your time!

Unfortunately as all adults know, time is the one thing we lose as we get more accustomed to and have more familiar sex with our partner. There is a tendency for us to 'take short cuts' between steps. Our personal sexual activities become so well-known and so well grooved we often skip the all-important kissing and foreplay, which were once the foundation of and a pleasurable "means and end" in itself. Busy adults quickly get telescoped and focused in on the actual entrée of sexual intercourse. Never do this! If you do, you are cheating your lady, yourself and your relationship of enormous and valuable sexual pleasures.

To demonstrate this, think back again to your teenage necking days and nights. You kissed for hours on end, again and again despite all the frustration and physical discomfort it entailed. Obviously the pleasures it gave you outweighed all you had to endure. Kissing can still give you that same kind of pleasure but this time without all the agony and 'blue balls' of the past, because now you have the added bonus of knowing it will not end in the frustration of having to stop. It will now end with both of you being completely satisfied and sexually satiated.

Your kissing session should completely mirror the cycle of your lovemaking; beginning with foreplay, progressing to sexual intercourse and ending with afterglow. Here's how this works: In the same way good and healthy foreplay starts out gentle, and teasing gradually works its way up to being more passionate and intense, so does good kissing. By kissing a woman in this mirrored image way your kisses give off a powerful non-verbal signal indicative of the way you will make love to her. It's as if your body language is saying to her, "This is how we will be when we are having sex, full of intense passion." This is an irresistible turn-on to any woman who wants to have great sex, which is every woman!

If you do it 'wrong' you are giving her just as clear a signal that you are an immature and inexperienced lover. For example, some men kiss so hard they press a woman's lips and mouth against her teeth, which can be very uncomfortable and disconcerting. Her focus is centered on the discomfort, not on you. This only serves to put her on early notice this is exactly the same way you will be thrusting your penis into her during sexual intercourse.

Unfortunately, despite what we may believe to be true as portrayed by the pornography industry, no woman in this type of sexual scenario is going to get much out of a violent sexual episode, except a cervical pounding and bruising, or vaginal soreness and abrasions. All of which do very little in the pursuit of satisfactory physical or mental sensations. Very rough and debilitating kissing is a turn-off for most women, except perhaps for those who are seriously masochistic.

Another common and ineffective kissing method is to kiss in exactly the same way each and every time. Same pressure, same duration, same lip contact, same tongue movements and penetration without any kind of variation. Again, this only shows and tells a woman that you are a very staid, ineffective and unimaginative lover. There are various and multiple ways of kissing badly, but you get the idea.

Here is a way to kiss her and continue to make progress on your path to her paradise patch. First, begin by kissing her gently and softly, barely brushing against her lips with yours. Once again remember, *take your time*.

As with the beginning of foreplay, kissing can be the most important stage of your lovemaking for her. At this point do not use your tongue, except perhaps to flick or stroke it very lightly on her lips to help moisten them. Soon your lips as well as hers will slowly grow passionately swollen and more sensitive (in the same way her genitals will, when you are kissing and licking them). Now she will want you to increase the pressure. *Don't do it!*

Continue to lightly kiss her lips while frequently moving your head to brush your lips and tongue across the skin of her neck, cheeks and ears. You should also lightly caress her with your fingers and hands but *only* above the shoulders.

After you have thoroughly teased her in this way you may now gently increase your lip pressure and begin to *slightly* insert the tip of your tongue into her mouth. Make light contact by flicking your tongue and teasing at the moist insides of her lips and on the tip of her tongue.

She will now open her mouth wider urging you to penetrate her mouth more deeply with your tongue. *Do not do it!* She will then try to put her tongue into your mouth. *Don't let her* do this either. If she tries, move your head slowly and gently caress other parts of her face, neck and shoulders with your lips or go back to stage one teasing. Your lead accomplishes two very important things; first, it will let her know that you are in control, which will be extremely exciting for her, and second she'll realize you won't be rushed. This sends a signal that if she tries to rush you, she will get even less than she wants. You may even want to whisper to her: "let's go slow", "take it easy", "we'll get there in plenty of time" or "relax and let me take care of your needs." Your voluntary restraint and attentiveness to caressing her with your lips and tongue will be explicit, exciting, and will drive her crazy. She will now realize there is no reason to hurry and your sole intention is to allow her to float on the air of your touch. Soon you will both be *very* excited and absolutely nothing has taken place below the neck.

Incidentally, this will be extremely erotic to her for three distinct reasons; first, she is not used to a man taking time with her and not trying to rush her into sexual intercourse. Second, women experience a gradual building of sexual excitement in a more upward curve than men do. And third, your movements undoubtedly will trigger for her memories of previous and past moments associated with the sweet torment of her sexual self-discovery from her youthful years in the back seat of that car on lovers' lane.

Now you may begin deep kissing her mouth (the symbolic equivalent for her of sexual intercourse.) However, you must continue to do this teasingly and sinuously. Slip your tongue into her mouth but keep the pressure of your lips light and soft. Consciously move your tongue in and around her mouth as if mimicking the gliding and sliding sensual motions of your penis, as it will be when the two of you begin to have sexual intercourse.
Slide your tongue in, out and around her mouth exploring every nook and cranny of her lips, teeth

and mouth. Let your tongue writhe and wriggle against hers. Then pause and gently pull away to kiss her face, neck and shoulders again for a while. Go back to deeply kissing her again, but more passionately this time. Now you may allow her to slide her tongue into your mouth (allowing her to mimic the woman-on-top position.)

She will definitely start to want more of you now. She will try to kiss you harder. She will start breathing deeper and may start gasping. Her hips will involuntarily begin moving up and down against you. Do not respond immediately, instead keep sensually kissing her. Do not touch her below the shoulders and do not allow her to touch you. If she tries to touch or her hands stray, keep her hands and arms in yours. Once again this will reinforce that you will not be rushed into sexual intercourse. This way you will slowly build her up to a level of utmost arousal.

At last she will be fully aroused. She will now be ready for her highest stage of heightened passion. Now your kissing can begin to mimic the final thrusting towards explosion and orgasm when movements become faster, harder and more intense. Kiss her passionately. Let her kiss you passionately. Let her give full vent to her excitement and heat. At this moment, begin sliding your hands down and around her body, touching her breasts, hips and genital area. If you were to enter her with your penis, she would probably reward you with a rapid series of powerful orgasms. But you are not going to enter her yet, no matter how much she may beg!

"Don't worry, it only seems kinky the first time."

~Author Unknown

Chapter 6: Foreplay As She Never Imagined
"Now, for below the belt foreplay."

Pleasure Technique # 2
The most important part of any sexual encounter is foreplay! The 'kissing above the shoulders stages' described previously, was the first phase of foreplay. If you have followed the previous steps, it will be a cinch for you to succeed in getting to and successfully preparing for the next phase; 'below the belt' foreplay.

You're probably already aware of this, but by remembering this one thing, you can bring your lady to sexual ecstasy. *A woman's clitoris is the key to her sexuality.* In fact, the word "clitoris" means "key" in Greek, but you knew that already, right? Here is what you might have not known; touch her clitoris before she is ready and she will think you are a clumsy fool. Touch her clitoris when she is ready and she will follow you anywhere and allow you to do anything.

To better understand why this is so, imagine a finger rubbing against the dry tip of your penis. Uncomfortable, right? It's the same for her. Clitoral stimulation too soon can be a problem. Not only is direct stimulation of her highly sensitive dry clitoris disconcerting and irritating, if a man persistently and repeatedly insists or tries to "hurry up" the sexual process, it can spell immediate 'cease and desist' of further sexual desires.

She may feel pressured to respond too quickly and as such she will not become adequately aroused or sufficiently lubricated. Pressure and anxiety to perform is as much the enemy of her arousal as it is for your pleasure. Without realizing it, a vicious cycle can start which may mean the end of your foreplay. If you fail to stimulate her enough it will take longer for her to reach orgasm (if she does at all). She may begin to associate sexual foreplay with you as frustrating instead of a new and exciting pleasurable experience. This is why the kissing technique described before is imperative to your successful encounter's continued foreplay 'below the belt.' The kissing technique guarantees she will be ready for you when you descend below the belt. You must stimulate her clitoris, not in order to arouse her, but *after* she is already aroused!

Now you may be asking, "How will I know when she is ready?" First, you must know when she is *not ready*! She is not ready when she is not adequately lubricated. Even if she is lubricated, she is *still* not ready if her genitals are not yet swollen. You may ask, "What must swell?" Answer, her vaginal lips;

both inner *and* outer. As well as the entire area around the entrance to her vagina and of course as a result, her clitoris. The key here is the more swollen, the better. The better lubricated and swollen she becomes the more readily available she will be for you to begin touching her clitoris and vaginal lips with your fingers or tongue. And the more ready she is for you, the more physical sensations she will feel from your touch, making her all the more open and responsive to you.

Don't worry, if you have taken the time to kiss and caress her correctly and long enough she will be ready. Sometimes however there is just not enough time to spend kissing (and to tell the truth, neither of you will want to every time).

What if she is not quite ready or lubricated enough? The best short cut to clitoral stimulation without irritation is to apply light indirect pressure first. If she is dressed, brush your fingers or palm of your hand lightly over her vulva outside her clothes. Then over her panties. Finally, over her skin. If she is already undressed, caress the vulva area through her robe or through the bed sheet. In this way even if she is not totally ready, your contact will not be irritating. The lighter your touch at this point the better. This will also help accelerate her excitement.

Again, a woman is *unlike* a man who wants his penis firmly grasped when he has an erection. She wants her clitoris to be touched delicately. She responds better to subtle and sensitive stimulation of her clitoris rather than direct pressure.

The next best way to circumvent the time issue in reaching maximum lubrication is to use lubricants. Start first with your tongue, lips and saliva, or some form of liquid vegetable oil or one of the many artificial lubricants available from your local drug store or pharmacy. Be sure you lubricate her genitals thoroughly before touching them with pressure.

Many women use indirect pressure on themselves when they masturbate, first by massaging their clitorises through and around their outer vaginal lips. It is only when they are at a peak of excitement that they usually begin to use more direct pressure to stimulate their clitorises. So do what they do, to and for themselves. Start with indirect stimulation.

You now have two ways to know if and when she is ready for more direct stimulation of her clitoris: She will let you know in no uncertain terms by either telling you or by putting your hands where she wants them, and/or her panties will be soaking wet. (As in all aspects of sexual life, there are exceptions. A woman may have insufficient self-lubrication production capabilities, even though she may be highly excited and stimulated due to menopausal or some other medical or physical circumstances.)

Here is something else you may not be aware of. Most women are more responsive to sexual intercourse *after* they have had an orgasm. As a woman she is naturally multi-orgasmic. For her, the first orgasm is exactly that; the first. If you don't believe this then you are thinking like a man. Once a man has ejaculated, he normally loses sexual interest fairly quickly and as such his sexual ability is generally finished for about twenty minutes minimally. Not so for her. Remember a woman is not like a man, so when you are finished it is the time to start stimulating her clitoris again. This time when you do, stimulate it directly and continue until she reaches orgasm again. As you are stroking her clitoris, pay attention to her breasts as well. There are few erotic sensations more intense for a woman than to have their nipples and clitoris stimulated simultaneously.

To really drive her crazy, stop and pause for a few seconds then start on her clitoris again, each time taking her to a higher level of excitement. Each time she is about to climax, no more teasing; keep your stimulation steady so she will not lose her peak. When she is ready for firm and stronger pressure on her clitoris she will let you know by straining her hips upward. Keep going with your hands, fingers, mouth or toys as she directs you, for each one will produce in her a different set of sensations (which she will delight in and crave again in the future). Each time, don't stop until she comes again!

Before her genital swelling subsides, now is the time to enter her with your penis. After you are finished this time and you have both come (together ideally), remember she may still be ready and able for you to continue stimulating her clitoris for additional orgasmic sensations, which she is able to have. Do So! Give her all she wants.

"I once knew a woman who offered her honor.
So I honored her offer.
And all night long I was on her and off her."

~Author Unknown

Chapter 7: Orgasms That Spoil Her for Any Other
"Finding her illustrious and elusive 'G Spot'."

Pleasure Technique #3
At this point you may be asking, "What about penis size and length?" Be reassuring, regardless of what the magazine articles say, the pornography industry promotes or the Internet spammers tell you, penis size really doesn't matter.

There are two God given reasons for this. First, vaginas are totally elastic. That is, they are designed to stretch and grasp tightly anything inserted into them. Whether an object is one half inch thick or three inches thick, four inches long or ten inches long, generally speaking they can accommodate any and all. And second, a woman's "G spot" (the source of her vaginal orgasms during intercourse) is a mere one to two inches inside her upper vaginal tract. Conveniently located where a penis of any size, length and girth can reach and easily pleasure. So realistically and objectively, any penis can and will do the job of adequately filling and satisfying any woman.

Subjectively she may think she prefers a larger penis, but if yours is the one giving her a sexual experience of total ecstasy and satisfaction every time you enter her, she will quickly become conditioned to expecting yours with hungered anticipation. It will be from you and you alone she comes to know and realize the levels of pleasure and desire she now needs, wants and craves. No matter your particular penis size, there is a way for you to imprint upon her memory and convince her there is no other partner anywhere who can make love to her and do what you can for her.

How is this possible? "It's not the size of the wand; it's the wizardry and talent of the magician." By recognizing and knowing it isn't so much what you do, as the way you do it, here are your new methods to use: The most important factor to remember; Readiness. If you have taken time to raise her to heights of excitement with swelling and wetness by giving her at least one clitoral orgasm, you are well on your way to establishing your place as the one man unique and special in her sexual life.

As her vagina swells, becoming extremely wet and receptive, you now enter her *slowly*. Slide deeply all the way in. The first push of the tip and head of your penis through the tautness of her vaginal entrance will be powerfully stimulating and exciting for her. After you are totally inserted deep inside of her, lie still for a moment so that she can experience your hardness and the shape of your penis' length throughout the entirety of her vagina. Allow her to have its full effect to enjoy in presence and pleasure.

Begin your first stroke with calm subtlety. Explore her vagina with your penis using short strokes and shallow jabs. Push the head of your penis against the different areas of her vaginal walls by moving in circular motions or back and forth movements while paying particular attention to her "G spot" area. Its location is on the forward upper wall about an inch or two from her vaginal entrance. To better access this infamous spot raise your body upright, sit on your butt with your crossed legs underneath and grasp her hips with your hands. Slightly lift her hips up and against you so that your penis will be positioned slightly forward and up against her "G spot" area. Move against her slowly and deliberately. If you continue to apply steady and firm friction to this spot, it will swell to hardening until she will ultimately experience an explosion of deep orgasmic pleasure. After she does, lie still but stay inside her. Allow her a minute to recover but do not withdraw your penis. During this time you may want to intensify her continued arousal through additional simultaneous stimulation of her clitoris and/or nipples. Do this, but keep your primary focus and intent on intercourse. Your goal and aim now is to transfer her other pleasure sensations to a single focal point again; her vagina.

Now, gradually begin to lengthen and deepen your strokes. By the time you reach this moment she will be completely at your mercy, so stay focused and concentrate on the pleasure *she* is experiencing. She will be bathed in the excitement of your penis to the exclusion of everything else. Her present reality will disappear and she will be lost in the faraway distance of her own enjoyment and ecstasy.

As she gets closer to reaching orgasm again she may begin to move with, or against you. Or she may lie completely still and allow you to take her to that place she alone sees in her mind. Know however that her mouth will not be still as she will not be able to stifle her moaning, her sounds of ecstasy or her pleas to you; "More, Harder, Deeper, Don't Stop, etc." Listen to her! At this point, she means what she says. Whatever else you do; do not change positions. Do not vary your strokes. Do not stop or pause. Keep going exactly the way you are and above all else, keep moving. If she responds with instructions or requests as to what she wants next, do it, but don't allow yourself to climax (more on this later).

After she has come and her orgasm begins to subside, be still but remain inside her. Look into her eyes, kiss her cheeks, ears, neck, face, forehead and wait for one minute. Then resume stroking her again slowly with your penis.

Change positions at this point if you want to; her on top, you from behind, whatever. She will be responsive and allow you to do as you wish. You will easily be able to withdraw and re-enter her immediately, for she will still be wet, hot and swollen. Gradually stroke more vigorously but keep a steady rhythm going. To her own surprise she will quickly be transported to her previous peak of excitement or even to a new and higher one. The next orgasm she experiences will be even more intense and more satisfying than the previous one.

If you are in a rear entry position ("doggy style") and if you are stroking her clitoris, she may push your hand away to better concentrate on her vaginal sensations. Or she may tell you, or take your hand and place it on her clitoris, or she may start stroking her clitoris with her own hand. Similarly she may pull your hands and fingers from her nipples or put them there. Whatever she wants, follow her lead!

Believe me, you can repeat this process indefinitely or until one, or both of you are physically exhausted. However it need not end, even then. Remember the female anatomy: the more orgasms she has, the more orgasmic she will become and the more orgasm episodes she can experience. As soon as you are able to have another erection, whether it is twenty minutes or two hours (or more) do it all over again. She will be ready and this time you can start with her clitoris, which will still be wet, swollen, highly sensitized and receptive to your lips, tongue or touch.

Although it is true both vaginal and clitoral orgasms involve contractions, clitoral orgasmic contractions are more localized and closer to the surface of the skin than vaginal ones. Vaginal orgasms are deeper and will often involve contractions of both the uterus and the pelvic muscles.

When the two of you are coupled in vaginal intercourse and her deep contractions begin, she is nearing orgasm. You can feel these contractions with the head of your penis if you are conscious of what is happening. At first her vagina will feel as if it is opening or enlarging as it is widening. When this happens, lighten up your strokes and shift your entire body a little further up on hers so that your penis rides against the top of her vaginal wall. Her vagina will seem to tighten up and close around your penis and it will feel as if she is trying to push you out. This is the time to increase both your speed and depth by going harder and faster. If you continue to repeat this action; lightening up when she loosens up and increase the pressure and your thrust when she tightens up, you will be able to take her to ever higher levels of ecstasy and wave after wave of orgasmic delight.

By the time you are done loving her, she will be in such a state of pleasurable bliss she will be completely respondent to the penis and person who put her there. You!

"Sex is just another form of talk,
where you act the words instead of saying them."

~D. H. Lawrence,
Lady Chatterley's Lover

Chapter 8: Increase Your Staying Power
"Remember that it is not essential that you be in a state of constant erection in order to give your lady great sex."

In order to achieve and please your sexual partner as previously described, you will need to maintain an erection for long periods of time. This need not be as taxing or as strenuous as it sounds. To understand this better remember sexual encounters have a life of their own. They have their own ebb and flow. They tend to swing back and forth between moments and phases of extreme intensity and subtlety, subsiding many times before they reach a climactic conclusion.

When you feel yourself building to an inevitable orgasm during sexual intercourse, you need to do two things. First, mentally take yourself out of your impending thoughts of where you are and what is about to happen (your exploding orgasm). Second, withdraw your penis and rest. Immediately replace your penis with your fingers, tongue, toys or other objects in order to allow your lady the opportunity to continue her escalation of excitement and pleasure.

Rest as long as you need but before going completely limp, reinsert yourself into her.

Do these as often as is necessary or as often as you wish. Don't worry, you can't hurt yourself and you can safely delay your release for a good long time. In many instances this will increase your pleasure, as well as hers. The only time you should avoid withdrawing from her is when she is about to or is having an orgasm, because at this point she will want and need you inside her to complete her orgasm and to be able to start building toward the next one. Make sure if you are going to withdraw and rest you do it before she gets to these moments of her building orgasmic release.

Once she has climaxed and is in what could be called her "hair-trigger orgasmic readiness" stage, she will be relatively indifferent as to the actual instrument inserted into her to reach orgasm again. If you and your penis have given out and are spent, you can use any penis shaped object to continue to please and pleasure her. What's most important is that *you* are still making love to her. It is simply a surrogate or substitute penis, which is doing the actual penetration. There are a multitude of different safe and acceptable objects available on the market today for your partner's enjoyment.

Without pharmacological or chemical assistance there is no way for you to continually keep a strong physical erection for hours on end, even if your lovemaking session itself goes on hour after hour. You must allow yourself to become relaxed when you need to rest and you must convey to your partner this does not mean you have lost your passion for her or the situation. When you do need to rest, do so, you can continue to please her with your fingers, hands, mouth and/or a variety of toys and other devices. If you keep pleasuring her sensually and easily, she won't feel deprived at all. Quite the contrary for you will further deepen your place in her heart and mind while imprinting and reinforcing the cascading thoughts of you, thoughts that she wants and craves more of you, thoughts of wanting to be with you, and refusal to be without you in either her life or her body.

After you have taken her to the new heights of excitement and ecstasy she is enjoying with you, she will be ready, willing and able to accept anything you want to do for and with her.

"We settle for so-so sex because most of us don't
know how sexual we could be;
we know only how sexual we are.
How sexual we are has been shaped by decades of
indoctrination, by family and friends, teachers,
religious leaders, and romantic partners, not to
mention a society that worships a bewildering
fusion of childlike sexual innocence and cynical,
nihilistic hedonism.

So what *is* normal?
It all depends on what's normal for *you.*"

~Anita H. Clayton,
*Satisfaction: Women, Sex,
and the Quest for Intimacy*

Chapter 9: For Committed Long Term Relationships

*"You and your partner may have honed your
lovemaking into a quick efficient routine."*

By now you have perhaps read, tried, practiced and
experienced the 'Three Pleasure Techniques.' As
you have seen, above all else they require time.
Chances are if you are currently in a long-term
committed relationship, you are both probably well
versed and knowledgeable as to what the turn-ons
are for each other. You do this. She does that. Then

onto the entrée, finis. How long does it all take? Ten, fifteen, twenty minutes, or less?

Understand there is nothing wrong with this kind of sex and as noted before, other responsibilities of daily life often encroach on what little time is left available for lovemaking and physical companionship. However, if this is the *only sex* the two of you are having, it could be grist for the mill of potential problems on the horizon.

If your lovemaking has turned into a continued repetition of the same routine, there is something inherently dangerous indeed. Not only does your predictability create a staid familiarity, with it can come boredom for either or both of you. This will begin to play upon her by evidence of decreased response to you. The time and intensity you once took and which was necessary for her arousal, excitement and which created her original sexual lusting for you may be waning or lost.

Re-read the steps of sexual lusting again and again until they become your lovemaking habit and you know them by heart. Go over them in your mind and mix in a variety of sexual fantasies and situations, which the two of you have discussed with each other in your moments of unabashed vulnerability.

Perhaps you've heard it said, "Variety is the spice of life." To help keep your love life alive it must be broad ranged and varied. So surprise her! Go away for a weekend, just the two of you. Pick a place without interruptions or distractions. A spot where the two of you can be together in an unhurried, unstressed and uncluttered environment. On the way, stop often and enjoy each other's company. Don't be in a hurry. Talk to each other about anything *other* than your normal daily life events and people. Make up scenarios of sexual intrigue to be played out when you reach your destination. Use your imaginations creatively. Take the time to make your hours together special again.

When you arrive and are comfortable, begin with the kissing technique and take your time! With the passing of years, family demands, occupational commitments and the onset of routine sex the two of you may have been experiencing, this will again seem new and exciting to her.

After a current relationship history of time pressured "quickies" she will undoubtedly be shocked and revitalized by your leisurely pace, so prepare her. Tell her with an eagerness and seductiveness you want to try something new. Tell her to completely relax and to let you take over. This in and of itself will be intensely exciting to her, for every woman enjoys the idea of relinquishing control and being taken and ravished by a powerful lover. By the time you have reached the final Pleasure Technique stage (Chapter 7) you will be like new lovers, rediscovering your passion as a couple.

If and when your sex life becomes rote and routine in the future you now have the opportunity to reinvent and reinvigorate your lovemaking experiences together.

"When she's having sex,
no woman remains grandiose."

~Elfriede Jelinek,
The Piano Teacher

Chapter 10: Sexual Enhancers
*"You have now reached the point where you can
enhance and refine your lovemaking with her."*

By now your lady is amazed and astounded by what
she is feeling from your uncanny sexual wisdom. To
her it may seem as if you have come to know her
body almost as well as she does. You and you alone
are able to arouse and satisfy her as if aware of her
most intimate thoughts, fantasies and desires. Who
could know such secrets about her female wants and
needs? She will now begin to trust and be more open
with you. She will grow to be ready and enthusiastic
in response to any and all offers of pleasure you
make.

It is here your sexual inventiveness, sensitivity and
openness become paramount in their importance.
One way to use her secrets and fantasies to arouse
and pique her interest is during the pre-physical
foreplay stage. That is, by whispering, talking and
suggesting verbally to her in public or in private
what she *might* expect from you later. Accompany
this with a touch, a kiss or an embrace and you will

start her wheels turning and moisten her vaginal area with great expectancy.

Turn-Ons and Fantasies
As you come to know your partner and her sexuality better, there are a number of ways by which you can replace hours of foreplay with more immediate arousal intensifiers. By sexually indulging her you will begin to gain her trust. When she reaches a point where she believes and trusts enough to open herself up, she will share with you her biggest sexual turn-ons so you can use them to instantly light the fire of excitement within her.

She is now conditioned to responding to you sexually, so just teasing reminders of what she might get from you later will arouse her. A touch of her nipple or brushing your hard and erect penis against her hand or leg will telegraph memories and images to her sexual circuitry and have her juices flowing. Do this kind of pre-physical foreplay often and regularly enough and she will always be ready to have you slip inside her, in private or in public.

One note of caution here; remember the importance of variety! Once you become privy to your lady's sexual secrets and fantasies don't use them routinely. Keep them for special moments or occasions and they will continue to give you a loving hold over your lady, which she will cherish and enjoy even more when you use them with her.

Here are some tips about sexual enhancers that will allow you both to perhaps step into uncharted waters of boundless creative lovemaking, which will further serve your new healthy lust for each other.

Fellatio

What about fellatio? What makes some women love it and others hate it? There is a secret to fellatio; women who love sexual intercourse usually enjoy fellatio. Conversely, women who hate fellatio usually don't enjoy intercourse or at least more often than not, they don't climax during intercourse. Here is the connection; fellatio and sexual intercourse in a sense is very much the same thing to a woman. Both acts consist of a penis entering her body and penetrating her.

If she dislikes or fears penetration, she will most likely not enjoy fellatio. Her mouth will be very tense and her throat very constricted. It is this fear and sense, which makes a penis in her mouth feel very suffocating and uncomfortable.

The way to help her overcome this fear and sensation and the way to get her to accept having your penis in her mouth is to get her to the point where she loves vaginal intercourse with you as described previously. As she learns to trust in you and begins to more consistently accept you into her vagina she will begin to do the same thing with her mouth. This is because she will begin to associate your penis with her total pleasure and satisfaction. She will start to enjoy it instead of fearing it and become less concerned about any discomfort. Her resistance will gradually fade away and she may soon learn that she enjoys being filled with you orally as much as she does vaginally.

Three important points of consideration here:
First, this transition may take time for her to adjust to, and be totally accepting of. Go slow, be patient and allow her to discover for herself what feels comfortable. *Do Not* expect her to immediately "Deep Throat" you. In fact, you will find light licking and stimulation from her tongue gently up and down the surface of your shaft can be as exciting as a raucous blowjob. The sensory nerves of your penis are located in, on and around the tip anyway. Why do you think they call it 'Head'? The more she is allowed to discover for herself, at her own pace, the sooner and more completely involved with oral sex she will become.

Second, *Do Not* insist (or even suggest) that she "swallow." Trust me on this one; one step at a time and you will both get to the finish line sooner. And third, if you don't ever go down on her, don't expect her to reciprocate full throttle whenever and wherever you want her to.
Pushing the Envelope
Nothing makes a woman want to please her man more than being pleased and appreciated for herself.

If you give of yourself as a lover totally devoted to her pleasure, she will be overwhelmingly desirous to do the same to and for you in return. Your passionate responses to her will be immensely gratifying and exciting and will give her a deep sense of sexual power. A power she will want to use over and over again, on and with you, to bring you to the brink of orgasm as often as she can and as often as you would like. It will become natural for her to do whatever, whenever and wherever you want. Your sexual wish will become her command because it will be her you are sharing it with.

If you want her to do something which she considers demeaning, such as anal sex, ménage a trios or having rear entry sex in front of a mirror while filming or recording the act, etc., be considerate. This is not a problem. Again, as trust in the relationship and in your sexual sharing grows and strengthens, leaps of faith can be made.

Remember she wants you just as much as you want her, although it may be new and uneasy for her (or you) at first. By discussing fully and openly before, during and after the event, the affection and appreciation which is built will allow you both to see sexual experimentation as exciting and in no way demeaning. If you both agree that anything you agree to is acceptable and if either says no, then no it is, new and fulfilling sexual inroads can be explored together and shared lovingly.

Menstruation

This is a good news/bad news scenario. First of all, if either one of you are adamantly against intercourse during her period for whatever reasons, enough said. However believe it or not, there is a window of opportunity within a woman's menstrual cycle when her hormones can go crazy and she may become sexually voracious. This is the good news. The bad news is it is different for every woman. This remains for the two of you to discover and act upon appropriately.

This "hot point" time can come right before or right after her period or in some women during it. Knowing when exactly takes careful observation. She may claim PMS symptoms but a large part of her PMS may actually be those out of control hormones clamoring to be satisfied.

If and when the two of you make love during these times her clitoris will be hypersensitive and she will be *very* wet. Her libido may also be at a heightened sense of uninhibited lasciviousness. This is your moment to work her into a frenzy and broach the subjects of fantasies and "outside the box" activities the two of you may have been discussing but as of yet have not acted upon. Biologically she may be more receptive to you at this time or perhaps even turned on by the very sexual possibilities the two of you have discussed back and forth in private.

Hormones

Just as hormones can make a woman very hot, they can also make her cold. When she is extremely unresponsive to your overtures she may still be approachable. The best way to accomplish this is to start with the kissing technique once again. When you start, assure her that you only want to kiss, hold and cuddle with her. Be sure to let her know you do not want, nor do you expect sexual intercourse. You simply want to kiss and hold her. No woman can refuse this. By the very way they have been designed and made, women have a greater tactile and sensual need than men do. In other words, women loved to be hugged and kissed, sex or no sex.

Most important here; make good on your word! This means you kiss her without trying to go any further, period. If she wants to stop, then you stop. When you consistently respect her wishes, this takes the pressure off and she can relax. When she knows that you mean what you say she will be more at ease to continue kissing and cuddling with you. You must still make no move to go further.

If you are patient and continue this long enough she will eventually become excited, although it may take much longer than usual. Wait for her to make the next move. She may, eventually.

Using Adult Movies with Even the Most Uptight Woman

Clinical and laboratory tests prove that women <u>in general</u> are just as stimulated and turned on by watching others having sex as men are. This has been shown over and over again in clinical trials where instruments are connected to the genitals to measure and record the amount of blood flow to the vaginal area while the subjects are exposed to adult movies. If you broach the subject and she agrees, make sure the first time you both select together what will be viewed. Try to choose something that is sensual and not degrading, weird or far out. Remember, general female population subjects of clinical studies and your lady may be very different in their tastes and applications of adult materials. *Do Not* force the issue upon her and be prepared to compromise.

"Once the buttons are undone,
you know how it'll all end.
It's all in the game, there are no miracles."

~Gao Xingjian,
Weekend Quartet

Chapter 11: Keeping Her Exclusively Yours
"Sex thrives on variation, surprise and expectation."

One of the most important things to know about sexual lusting and its success for you, your partner, your sex life and your relationship is to avoid the danger of "automatic sex." That is, do not have sex the same way each and every time. This is the nemesis and bane of all long-term relationship sex and can be the death-knell of any individual's or couple's sex life.

There is nothing more exciting to a woman than when you change the licking or stroking methods and patterns you use on her clitoris. Try it! Stroke her clitoris in a pleasurable way giving her moments and pulsations of excitation then change the stroke entirely. Alter the rhythm; make it faster or slower. Change your touch; making it lighter or firmer or explore an entirely different area altogether. See if she doesn't respond positively and moan her acceptance as you do

If your sex life seems in danger of getting stale or is sliding into familiar territory return to using the principles stated previously. Stop taking 'short cuts.' Go back to the basics (Chapters 4, 5, 6 & 7). Go back to kissing and teasing. Kiss and tease her over and over again in spurts, starts and stops all day long but don't let her climax until nightfall.

Also remember to have some serious sexual marathons again. Bring her once more to her highest level of ardor and sustained pleasure that addicted her to you in the first place. Touch her in unexpected ways and often. Reveal to her a secret desire or fantasy of yours, which you have kept hidden deep within you. This will put you once again back under her power.

Above all else remember that sexual pleasure once having been experienced can always be repeated, intensified and enjoyed yet again.

"I think it's funny that we were freer about
sexuality in the 4th century B.C.
It is a little disconcerting."

~Angelina Jolie,
Interview, Nov. 22, 2004

Chapter 12: Seven Keys for Lovemaking Success

"Here are seven key things to remember about sensuality, sexuality and lovemaking."

- ❖ Sensuality, sexuality and lovemaking are cornerstones of human intimacy.

- ❖ Everything in sexuality is attitude, belief and perception.

- ❖ Sexual encounters are heightened and enhanced when you intimately want to please your partner more than yourself.

- ❖ The most important sexual organ in your body is your mind.

- ❖ Stay physically fit. Understand that extended/marathon sex is an exercise in aerobics.

- ❖ It's not the size of the wand; it's the wizardry and talent of the magician.

(Size matters only as a visual stimulation. To make your penis appear and seem larger, shave yourself all the way to the base.)

❖ Foreplay feeds the mind, intercourse feeds the body, holding her afterward feeds the soul.

This ends "Seduction, Pleasing Women Sexually." I hope you have enjoyed, learned and practiced. Now, Keep It Up!

Epilogue

Every man believes he's a good lover. But how does he know? Most men actively use on the adult women they are romantic with, the 'tried and true' lovemaking techniques they learned in their formative teen years. One important fact to remember here is, when hormones are raging, a young man's focus remains primarily on getting his penis stroked to ejaculatory climax by a willing partner's hands, mouth, or other penetrable orifices. Many men today are unconcerned as to any reciprocal pleasure which their partner may desire or enjoy. This is neither the correct attitude nor repertoire of a great, or even good lover. If you will learn and practice the advice and techniques presented herein you will become a great lover, but how will you know?

Remember, sex is mental first and most often. The most active sex organ in every human body is a creative and fantasies producing mind. Second, enjoy and extend your foreplay time and pleasures as much and as often as possible. Make touching, caressing, suggestive words, notions and ideas a continuous and on-going presence every time you are near your partner. Not only does foreplay set every romantic stage, it also heightens every sensual or sexual nuance which precedes or follows. Make your lovemaking sessions complete mind, body, and soul experiences.

Keep in mind that your partner's entire being, can be a sexually charged receptacle. Bring to bear through your actions and words, knowledge of your partner's needs and desires. The partners of great lovers *always know* they are the focus of the amorous advances from their lover.

It has been said, "Variety is the spice of (a great love) life." In a monogamous relationship this is just as true as in one with many different partners. The variety for couples is in keeping your partner guessing as to when, how and where your loving inclinations may be coming from next.

How will you know if you're a great lover?
Your partner will know. And she'll be sure to let you know. How? She'll always be ready for more of your lovemaking prowess; anyway, anywhere, and anytime you want.

Branch Isole is the author of nineteen books. Born in Osaka Japan, Branch Isole traveled extensively growing up calling many places home. Finishing high school in Rolling Hills, California he went on to graduate from Texas State University San Marcos, attended graduate school at the University of Houston and received an M.A. Theology degree from Trinity Bible College and Seminary, Newburgh Indiana.

Branch Isole's catalogue of work includes books, eBooks, greeting cards, inspirational gift mats, available at:

www.branchisole.com
www.manaopublishing.com

Other books by Branch Isole:

Erotica Series

Orgy of Words ©
Salacious Short Stories in Poetic Prose
ISBN 978-0982658529
eBook ISBN 978-0983574569

Poetic Prose Series

Epigram ©
long story short
ISBN 978-0982658574
eBook ISBN 978-0983574576

Heartstrings of Illusion ©
Distractions and Deceit in Poetic Prose
ISBN 978-0982658543
eBook ISBN 978-0983574545

Dreams and Schemes ©
Tales and Tattles in Poetic Prose
ISBN 978-0982658550
eBook ISBN 978-0983574552

In The Margins ©
where truth lies
ISBN 978-0982658536
eBook ISBN 978-0983574538

Eclectic Electricity ©
unknown poet's parade
ISBN 978-0982658512
eBook ISBN 978-0983574521

Turn Of A Phrase ©
Pivotal Positions in Poetic Prose
ISBN 978-0982658505
eBook ISBN 978-0983574514

Saccharin and Plastic Band Aids ©
Comments in Poetic Prose
ISBN 978-0974769288
eBook ISBN 978-0983574453

Messages In A Bottle ©
Inspirations in Poetic Prose
ISBN 978-0974769295
eBook ISBN 978-0983574446

Reflections On Chrome ©
Parking Lot Confessions in Poetic Prose
ISBN 978-0974769257
eBook ISBN 978-0983574422

Postcards from the Line of Demarcation ©
Points of Separation in Poetic Prose
ISBN 978-0974769264
eBook ISBN 978-0983574439

Seeds of Mana'o ©
Thoughts, Ideas and Opinions in Poetic Prose
ISBN 978-0974769219
eBook ISBN 978-0983574415

Barking Geckos ©
Stories and Observations in Poetic Prose
ISBN 978-0974769226
eBook ISBN 978-0983574408

Orgy of Words ©
Salacious Short Stories in Poetic Prose
ISBN 978-0982658529
eBook ISBN 978-0983574569

Spiritual Christianity Series

Even Christians Stumble and Fall ©
Musings of a Struggling Believer
ISBN 978-0974769240
eBook ISBN 978-0983574491

Crucibles ©
Refinement of the Neophyte Christian
ISBN 978-0974769233
eBook ISBN 978-0983574484

Power of Praise ©
Poetry of Spiritual Christianity ™
ISBN 978-0974769271
eBook ISBN 978-0983574477

GOD. . . i believe ©
Simple Steps on the Path
of Spiritual Christianity ™
ISBN 978-0974769202
eBook ISBN 978-0983574460

Self Help Series

Pathways to Publishing ©
Self Publishing
Manuscript to Publication
ISBN 978-0982658567
eBook ISBN 978-0983574507

GOD. . . i believe ©
Simple Steps on the Path
of Spiritual Christianity ™
ISBN 978-0974769202
eBook ISBN 978-0983574460

Seduction ©
Pleasing Women Sexually
ISBN 978-0982658598
eBook ISBN 978-0983574583